Australia's Environmental Issues

NATURAL DISASTERS

Redback Publishing
PO Box 357 Frenchs Forest NSW 2086
Australia

www.redbackpublishing.com.au
orders@redbackpublishing.com.au

978-1-925860-28-3

Author: Peter Turner
Editor: Michael Anderson
Proofer: Marianne Lindsell
Designer: Redback Publishing

Original illustrations © Redback Publishing 2019
Originated by Redback Publishing

Reprinted 2022
Printed and bound in Malaysia

Acknowledgements
Abbreviations: l—left, r—right, b—bottom, t—top, c—centre, m—middle
We would like to thank the following for permission to reproduce photographs: (Images © shutterstock) p22t English Wikipedia user Billbeee [GFDL (http://www.gnu.org/copyleft/fdl.html) or CC-BY-SA-3.0 (http://creativecommons.org/licenses/by-sa/3.0/)], via Wikimedia Commons, p22m By en:User:Billbeee [GFDL (http://www.gnu.org/copyleft/fdl.html), CC-BY-SA-3.0 (http://creativecommons.org/licenses/by-sa/3.0/) or CC BY 2.5 (https://creativecommons.org/licenses/by/2.5)], via Wikimedia Commons,

Every effort has been made to contact copyright holders of any material reproduced in this book. Any omissions will be rectified in subsequent printings if notice is given to the publisher.

A catalogue record for this book is available from the National Library of Australia

CONTENTS

INTRODUCTION

A natural disaster is a devastating event that is nevertheless a part of the rhythm and forces that shape our planet. Natural disasters cause great destruction, and threaten or take the lives of people and animals. Natural disasters can affect whole ecosystems, and throughout the history of Earth, they have shaped the way it looks and determined the success or failure of species that inhabit it.

Natural Disasters in Australia

Over time, Australia has experienced natural events that have helped to create the land we recognise today. For example, the dry, desert inland was once a vast sea, teeming with life. Today, that same area supports life of a very different kind. In Australia, the natural disasters that play an unpredictable part in all our lives are drought, fires, tropical cyclones, floods and, to a lesser extent, earthquakes. Each of these disasters affects us all, either directly or indirectly. We might suffer personal tragedy as a result of a natural disaster, or we might be affected economically as the food we take for granted suddenly becomes scarce and expensive.

Natural disasters remind us that we live in the natural world, that we are a part of it and that we are subject to its forces. Understanding this helps us to prepare, to protect and to recover.

ADAPTATIONS AND NATURAL DISASTERS

Some species have adapted to the environment and now rely on natural disasters for survival. Some Australian plants, for example, need the fierce heat and smoke of a bushfire in order to germinate and regenerate. Some trees need regular flooding to keep them healthy and to encourage them to flower.

CLIMATE CHANGE

Scientists now know that the Earth is experiencing more severe weather events because of human activity. Greenhouse gases, emitted by industries and our environmental practices, have caused global warming, and this has led to climate change. The consequences are far-reaching. The severity and frequency of floods, droughts and storms is likely to increase if the world fails to act.

HELPING SHAPE A NATION

Natural disasters in Australia have become an important part of our social history. Some, such as Cyclone Tracy, the Ash Wednesday bushfires and the Newcastle earthquake, are familiar to almost everybody in Australia. Disasters show us at our best and at our worst. They shape the landscape, and they help to shape our sense of ourselves as a nation.

TYPES OF NATURAL DISASTERS

TORNADO

A vortex of wind in the shape of a funnel that can cause a lot of damage

HAIL

Chunks of ice that fall during a storm or rain

TSUNAMI

Huge waves caused by an earthquake or volcanic eruption

LANDSLIDE

When a mountain or cliff face collapses

BUSHFIRE

A fire in grass, bush or woodland that is difficult to control

EARTHQUAKE

When the earth's crust moves and violently shakes

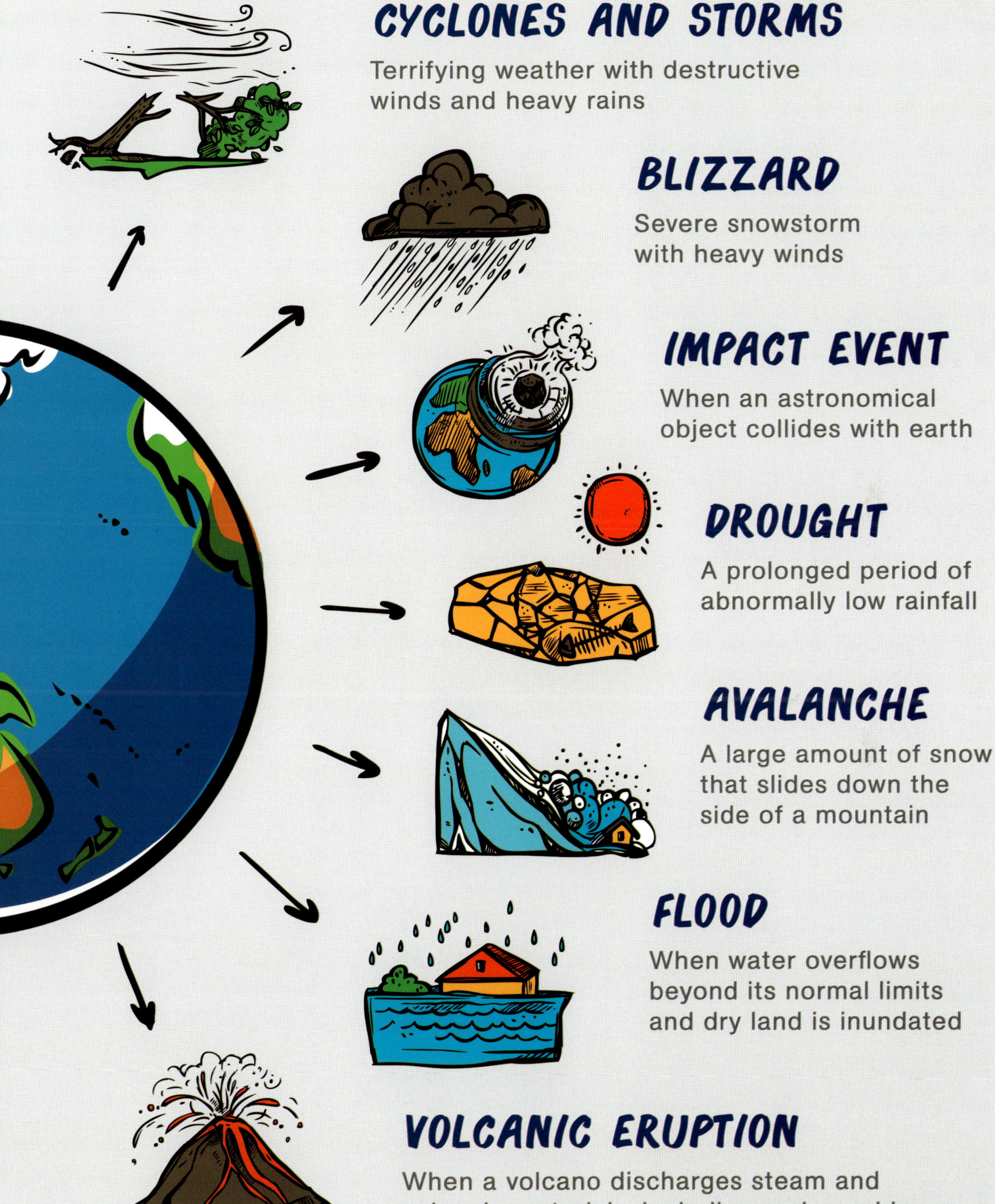

CYCLONES AND STORMS

Terrifying weather with destructive winds and heavy rains

BLIZZARD

Severe snowstorm with heavy winds

IMPACT EVENT

When an astronomical object collides with earth

DROUGHT

A prolonged period of abnormally low rainfall

AVALANCHE

A large amount of snow that slides down the side of a mountain

FLOOD

When water overflows beyond its normal limits and dry land is inundated

VOLCANIC ERUPTION

When a volcano discharges steam and volcanic materials, including rocks and lava

MANAGING NATURAL DISASTERS

A community that is well prepared for natural disasters is more likely to be well equipped to deal with one when it occurs. A well-prepared community is also better able to deal with the consequences of the disaster.

Drought

The Australian Bureau of Meteorology, along with the World Meteorological Organization, monitors weather patterns and contributes to the Climate Information and Prediction Services (CLIPS). This service aims to give advanced warning of potential droughts. It is not possible to make Australia drought-proof, but there are water-saving measures that can help to reduce the demand on reservoirs. Having shorter showers, more efficient showerheads, recycling greywater, installing rainwater tanks in gardens and fixing dripping taps all help. Governments introduce water restrictions in time of drought in order to cut down household usage. In rural areas, planting trees can help to stop the topsoil from blowing away, and covering irrigation channels can reduce evaporation. Australians should expect to experience drought regularly, and should always be conscious of how they use water, even when it seems there is plenty of it available.

WATER RESTRICTIONS IN EFFECT

BUSHFIRES

The CSIRO, the Department of Defence and Geoscience Australia have developed an Internet-based satellite tracking system called Sentinel Hotspots. This system allows people to see where a fire has started and where it is headed. Firefighting organisations use Sentinel Hotspots to locate and manage fires. Governments enforce days of total fire ban when conditions are very hot and dry. On total fire ban days, no fires may be lit in the open, and equipment that produces sparks cannot be used. People who live in or near the bush, and in towns, should ensure they have cleared up around their house and cleaned their gutters of leaves and twigs. They should also have a fire plan and be well prepared if they intend to stay and defend their property.

FLOODS

Flood warnings are issued for some floods. Warnings give people time to move to higher ground and to prepare their homes for flooding. It is difficult to give advanced warnings of flashfloods. People should have an evacuation plan if there is any danger of flooding in their area. When a flood warning is issued, gas and electricity should be shut off at the point where they enter the property, valuable items should be placed up high and heavy objects such as refrigerators should be opened. This is to stop them from floating and being damaged, or causing damage. People should have a portable radio (no electricity is available during a flood) to which they stay tuned to hear advice on rising floodwaters. They should never attempt to swim or drive through flood waters. After a flood, all drinking water should be boiled until the water supply is made safe.

EARTHQUAKES

Earthquakes happen so quickly that people make the mistake of rushing outside. Here, they become vulnerable to falling powerlines, crashing debris and flying glass. If you are indoors, stay there and shelter away from windows, under a doorframe or a table. If you are outside, move away from powerlines, buildings, walls and trees. Wherever you are, look up. If you are under a fan, ceiling light, shelf or any structure that might be shaken loose, move away.

DROUGHT

In Australia, drought is a natural consequence of the continent's geographical position. A drought occurs when an unusually long period of low rainfall results in there not being enough water to meet the normal needs of agriculture and of the community. Since Australia is the driest inhabited continent in the world, there is more to a drought than simply dry conditions. In many parts of Australia, low rainfall is perfectly normal. These places are not in a constant state of drought. They are simply experiencing the natural conditions of their climate.

How do we Know When There is a Drought?

In 1965, the Australian Bureau of Meteorology began a Drought Watch service, and in 1992 the Australian Government created new initiatives in its National Drought Policy. Together, these services determine when an area is in drought.

The Bureau of Meteorology keeps track of rainfall records throughout Australia. In any three-month period, if the Bureau notices that in a particular region the rainfall is below 10 per cent of what records show it should be, that region is placed on a Drought Watch. Of course, whether or not the area is in an arid region, and whether or not that region is normally dry during that period, are taken into account. The Drought Watch ends when average or above-average rainfalls return.

HOW DO WE KNOW IT IS A DROUGHT?

Low rainfall is only one of the conditions necessary for a drought to be declared. For example, a period of low rainfall may not lead to a drought if the region's water storages (dams and reservoirs) are full because of periods of good rainfall. However, a drought will occur when there is no relief from dry conditions, and water storages begin to fall sharply. This is a problem because, in hot weather, evaporation rates are high in water storages, and people want to use more water to keep their gardens alive. Farmers will need to use greater quantities of water to irrigate their crops.

When the state or territory government is advised that water storages are running low, and that a longer than usual period of low or no rainfall has developed, it declares that an area is in drought. The government then puts into place measures to reduce water usage, and farmers become eligible for drought relief because of loss of their crops or livestock.

HOW LONG DOES A DROUGHT LAST?

It is impossible to predict with any certainty how long a drought is likely to last. Some droughts can last for many years, while others might be short, but severe and intense. Both long-term and short-term droughts can cause great hardship and economic and environmental losses. Given Australia's size, it is often the case that drought will occur in one region, while another will be receiving plenty of rain. The drought of 1982-1983 was unusual in that it was widespread and affected most of Australia at the same time.

CAUSES OF DROUGHT

Periods of drought are a normal part of Australia's climate. This is because the continent is situated at a latitude in which the weather is strongly influenced by the subtropical high pressure belt. The subtropical high exists in both the Southern and Northern Hemispheres, in regions north and south of the Equator. The effect of a subtropical high is to create areas of warm, dry air, clear skies and not much rainfall. In some parts of Australia, other influences have an effect on the subtropical high and produce good rainfall for at least part of each year. This is the case in the far north, the far south and along the east coast. Elsewhere in Australia, though, the subtropical high means that rainfall remains low.

El Niño

A weather pattern known as the El Niño Southern Oscillation occurs in the Pacific region but has an effect on weather in many parts of the world. El Niño, which means 'the boy' in Spanish, is a warm ocean current that moves through the Pacific Ocean every three to eight years and is accompanied by changes in air pressure and sea temperature. As the current moves, the air pressure above it drops, and rain-bearing winds fail to arrive over land. El Niño can create drought over northern and eastern Australia. A severe El Niño event can create even more widespread drought, although the Australian Bureau of Meteorology says that droughts in the western and central parts of Australia usually have different causes.

NORMAL YEAR

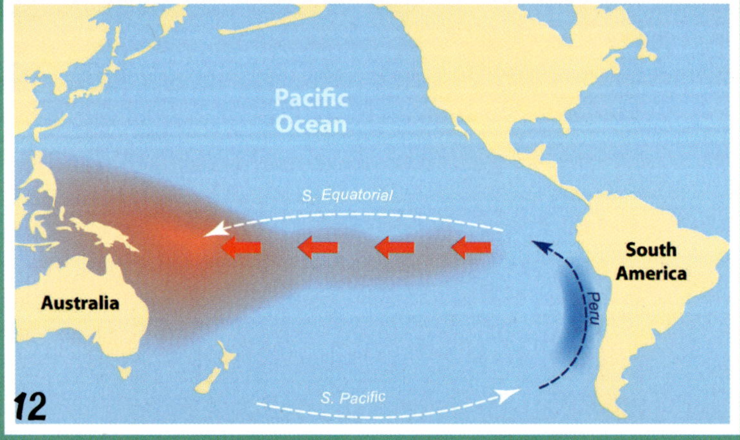

EL NIÑO YEAR

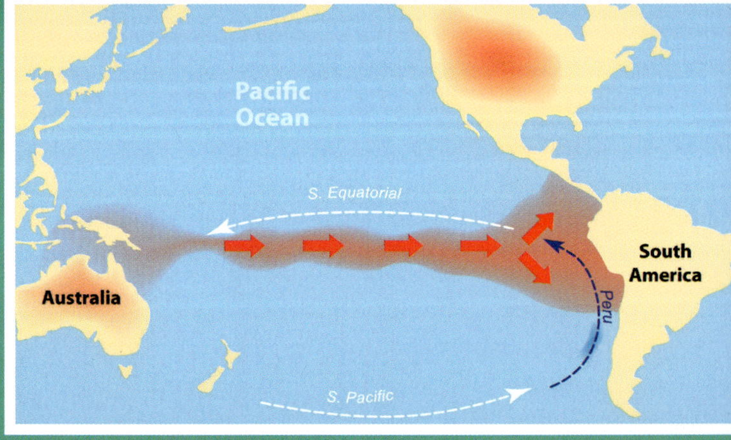

Melbourne Dust Storm

Small dust storms occur frequently during very dry periods, but the El Nino event of 1982-1983 created especially dry conditions. Strong winds picked up loose soil in the Wimmera and Mallee districts of western Victoria, and drove it in a huge, dark cloud across the state. The dust cloud reached Melbourne just before 3.00 pm on 8 February 1983, and completely engulfed the city. The Mallee district was left with bare earth, which made the effects of the drought even more severe there.

THE EFFECTS OF DROUGHT

Drought affects everyone and everything, especially farmers. Australia's economy is badly affected by a drought. Other problems include:

- Plants wither and die.
- Rivers, creeks and dams dry up.
- Soil turns to dust.
- Without food or water, wildlife is threatened and breeding cycles are interrupted.
- Crops fail.
- Farm animals no longer have nutritious grass on which to graze. In severe drought, tens of millions of sheep and cattle die.
- Farmers suffer both personal and financial hardship.
- For the rest of the community, it means an increase in the cost of food and the need to conserve water.
- Droughts increase the risk of bushfires.
- Droughts also create conditions in which the soil is so dry that high winds can produce dust storms. Dust storms are devastating because they blow away valuable topsoil, this is the rich fertile soil in which crops grow.

DROUGHT CASE STUDIES

From their first arrival in 1788, the first European settlers began observing that drought was a part of Australia's climate. In 1791, just three years after his arrival, Governor Arthur Phillip wrote: 'From June until the present time so little rain has fallen that most of the runs of water in the different parts of the harbour have been dried up for several months, and the run which supplies this settlement is greatly reduced.'

The Federation Drought, 1895-1902

The Federation Drought is one of the most severe and devastating droughts in Australian history. It is called the Federation Drought because it was at its worst during 1901 and 1902, when Australia became a federation.

The Federation Drought was severe because, for a few years before the very dry period, rainfall had been low. This was particularly true over most of Queensland and New South Wales. Victoria, too, had experienced lower than average rainfall.

In 1900, good rain fell in most parts of Australia that were expecting it, except for Queensland. These rains brought some relief, but in the spring of 1901 an intense dry period began over the eastern part of Australia. The consequences were dramatic.

In Queensland, the Darling River, one of the state's largest rivers, almost dried up. Many other rivers dried as well. Stock (sheep and cattle) losses were huge. Nearly 50 per cent of the sheep population and nearly 40 per cent of the cattle population died. Almost the entire Australian wheat crop was lost. It is difficult to estimate what these losses meant for the Australian economy.

There were other terrible consequences, too. The personal hardships suffered by people get lost among all the facts and figures. A farmer whose crop fails, or who loses livestock, faces economic ruin. This, of course, affects the farmer's family as well. It also affects the people and businesses the farmer supplies, those who supply the farmer with feed and equipment and the people who process the farmer's goods. Prices rise as food becomes scarce, and people find it more difficult to feed their families.

The Federation Drought led the Australian Government to consider ways of using irrigation more efficiently. It took until 1914, however, for a commission to be set up to examine how the Murray River might be used to irrigate the land through which it flowed.

OTHER DEVASTATING DROUGHTS

Drought occurs regularly in Australia. The droughts brought to Australia by the El Niño weather pattern are usually of short duration. However, between 1991 and 1995, the longest El Niño drought on record took place. This drought affected many parts of Australia, but it was most severe in Queensland and northern and eastern New South Wales. Rain fell during this period, sometimes causing floods, but the rainfall was always followed by intense periods of dry. The economic consequences were great. It is estimated that farmers lost almost $2 billion, and the economy as a whole lost $5 billion. Many farmers lost their farms. This drought also led to the terrible bushfires that swept through New South Wales and threatened Sydney in January 1994.

The worst drought this century occurred between 2003 and 2012, with certain parts of Queensland returning to a drought state in 2013–2014.

BUSHFIRES

Bushfire is not always disastrous because it can play an important role in the healthy life cycle of forest ecosystems. Many Australian native trees and shrubs depend on fire and smoke to create the right conditions for their seeds to germinate.

The Australian bush generally recovers well after fire. Unless a bushfire is particularly intense or is moving at great speed, native Australian animals can protect themselves by burrowing, or outrunning the flames. A bushfire becomes a natural disaster when it sweeps through areas that are inhabited by people, destroying property and crops, and taking lives.

How Bushfires Start

Bushfires may be lit deliberately or accidentally, as in lighting strikes. However they begin, they need the right atmospheric conditions, and the right fuel, to take hold and rage out of control. The Australian bush becomes vulnerable to fire when prolonged periods of dry weather leave large quantities of dry, inflammable fuel, such as leaves, twigs, sticks, bark and dead bushes, on the forest floor. The dominant tree in the Australian bush is the eucalypt, and its leaves have a high level of oil. This makes them highly flammable, especially when there is little moisture in the air.

CROWNING

In particularly fierce bushfires, the fire moves at great speed by leaping from the burning crown, or top, of one tree to another. This is called 'crowning', and is the most dangerous type of bushfire. These fires are bombed from the air, using aircraft to drop fire suppressants or water to douse them.

HOW BUSHFIRES IMPACT AUSTRALIA

The most devastating effects of bushfire are loss of life and destruction of people's homes. Fierce bushfires leave nothing in their wake. They are terrifying to experience, and if the conditions are right, they can explode upon people with astonishing suddenness. In high winds, and with dry, heated air, embers from a fire front can be blown well ahead and set an area alight that is some distance away from the main fire.

Firefighters understand how bushfires move, and often they will fight fire with fire, deliberately burning an area in its path, so that when the fire reaches an already burned area, there is no fuel allowing it to continue. This can only be done if there are no high winds. Fierce winds can blow fires in directions that cannot be predicted.

Bushfires can pollute the water supply by dumping ash and soot into reservoirs. It puts vast quantities of smoke into the atmosphere, lowering air quality. In 2006, Melbourne experienced several days shrouded in heavy smoke from fires burning out of control in alpine regions. People with breathing problems such as asthma were advised to stay indoors.

TIMELINE OF AUSTRALIA'S MAJOR BUSHFIRES

There are hundreds of bushfires in Australia each year. Some of them occur in remote areas, and some of them are much closer to where people live. From time to time, bushfires have been so extreme that they have had a disastrous effect on the lives of many people, and have caused the whole nation to feel some of the horror that attends such tragedies.

1926

JANUARY TO MARCH

Over 1,000 properties in Victoria were either destroyed or damaged and 60 people killed during a series of major bushfires, including the most devastating on February 14, which later became known as Black Sunday.

1939

13TH JANUARY

The Black Friday bushfires in Victoria were among the worst natural bushfires (wildfires) in the world. Almost 20,000 km² (4,942,000 acres, 2,000,000 ha) of land was burned and several towns were destroyed and 71 people died.

1943-44

The summer of 1943–44 was the driest summer ever recorded in Melbourne and numerous bushfires devastated areas of Victoria during this period. A year later, the Country Fire Authority was established to co-ordinate rural fire brigades.

1967

17TH FEBRUARY

110 separate fire fronts raged through southern Tasmania killing 62 people and injuring 900 more. Over seven thousand people lost their homes and an estimated 62,000 farm animals were killed. The event came to be known as Black Tuesday.

1969

JANUARY

Once again parts of Victoria were devastated by bushfire, with 23 people dead and 230 homes destroyed.

1983

ASH WEDNESDAY

In 1982-1983, eastern Australia experienced an intense, short drought as a result of a very dry El Niño event following a period of low rainfall. Conditions were perfect for outbreaks of fire. On 16 February a series of fires broke out, some deliberately lit, that caused widespread destruction across South Australia and Victoria. By the time the fires had died down a few days later, 75 people were dead — 47 in Victoria and 28 in South Australia. In one tragic incident, 17 firefighters lost their lives in the Dandenong Ranges, when high winds caused the fire to surround them.

1998

LINTON BUSHFIRE

Five volunteer firefighters died in the 1998 Linton bushfire. Their deaths led to changes in safety operating procedures in South Australia's Country Fire Service and Victorian Country Fire Authority.

2003

CANBERRA, 18TH JANUARY

Fires, possibly started by lightning strikes, broke out in Kosciuszko National Park and Namadgi National Park, close to the city of Canberra. It was soon clear that the high winds would fan these fires into a serious threat, and on 18 January the flames were driven into the Canberra suburbs. The ferocity of the fire took people completely by surprise, and it moved with terrifying speed. Four people died, and more than 530 homes were destroyed, with losses of more than $250 million. Almost 99 per cent of Namadgi National Park was destroyed, as well as 30 farms, the historic Mount Stromlo Observatory, large pine plantations and parkland.

2005

VICTORIAN BUSHFIRES

Four people died along with the loss of hundreds of homes and farm buildings, and over 65,000 farm animals.

2009

BLACK SATURDAY BUSHFIRES

Australia's worst ever bushfires began around 7 February 2009 and resulted in Australia's highest ever loss of life from a bushfire. 173 people died, another 400 were injured, and over 2,029 homes destroyed.

TROPICAL CYCLONES

Tropical cyclones – also called 'hurricanes' or 'typhoons' – are strong storms that develop over the ocean in regions that are close to the tropics. They are different from other storms in that they spin, gathering speed as they do so. A satellite photograph shows that a cyclone looks like a swirling mass of cloud, with a central point, called the 'eye'. The word 'cyclone' comes from a Greek word meaning 'wheel' or 'coil of a snake'.

Where Are Australia's Cyclone Areas?

The Australian Bureau of Meteorology estimates that, on average, ten tropical cyclones form in the oceans off the coast of north-western and north-eastern Australia each cyclone season. The cyclone season in Australia is between November and May. Of these 10 cyclones, six will probably make landfall. Cyclones can affect the weather patterns over much of Australia and can influence rainfall as far south as Victoria, but the areas most likely affected by tropical cyclones are:

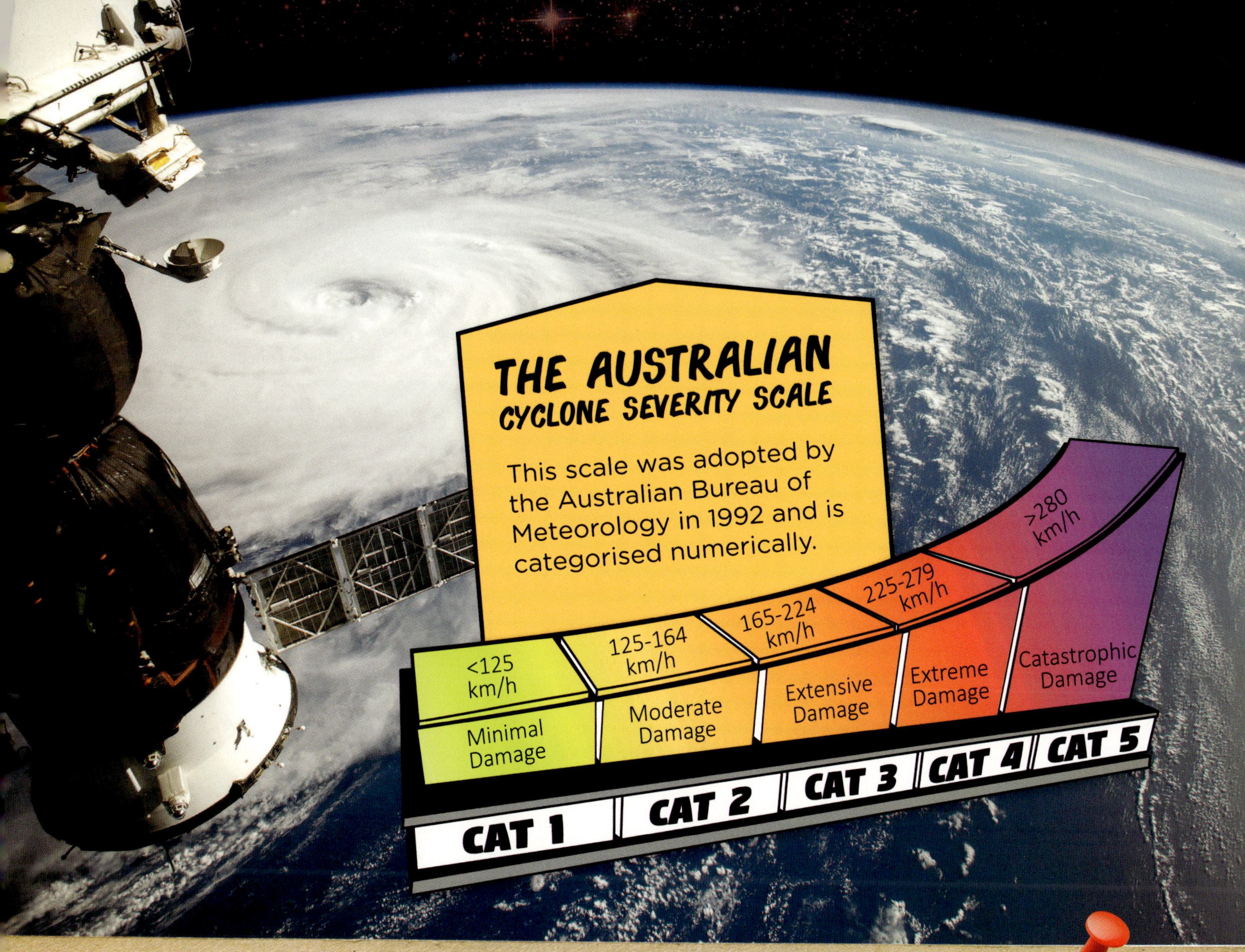

THE IMPACT OF CYCLONES ON AUSTRALIA

Tropical cyclones are a terrifying weather phenomenon because of their destructive winds and heavy rains. When Cyclone Vance struck the Pilbara region of Western Australia on 22 March 1999, a record wind gust of 267 kilometres per hour was recorded. Cyclone Vance was one of the most powerful cyclones ever to reach the coast.

Cyclones are at their most powerful out over the ocean and close to the coast. As they move inland, they begin to lose energy. However, they bring with them flooding rains, destructive winds and storm surges that can threaten coastal communities with sudden rises in the sea level.

Satellites and weather-tracking devices have made it possible to issue warnings ahead of a cyclone's development and to see where it is at a particular time. This is especially useful for the shipping industry. However, cyclones move in unpredictable directions. At one moment they might appear to be passing safely offshore, while at the next they might change direction and head inland.

Cyclones become natural disasters when they cause loss of life and property in communities. They are a part of the natural weather cycle, and are responsible for providing large parts of Australia with essential rain.

TROPICAL CYCLONE CASE STUDIES

Communities in Australia have regularly endured the destructive force of tropical cyclones. In 1899, 300 people died during a cyclone at Bathurst Bay, in northern Queensland. Before the advent of weather-tracking systems and good communications equipment, ships out at sea and coastal communities were vulnerable. Even with modern satellites and communications systems, cyclones can still have devastating consequences.

Cyclone Tracy, 1974

On Christmas morning in 1974, Cyclone Tracy swept through the capital of the Northern Territory, Darwin. Before this cyclone had moved through and blown itself out, it destroyed most of Darwin's buildings and killed 49 people in the town and 16 at sea.

Cyclone Tracy was not a particularly large cyclone, but the winds it generated were very strong. Tracy was a slow-moving cyclone, and the winds generated blew in Darwin for more than five hours. Darwin's buildings were not constructed to withstand such forces, and most of them collapsed. When the rest of Australia saw images of Darwin after Cyclone Tracy the most common response was that it looked as if a large bomb had been dropped on the town.

Cyclone Tracy was such a catastrophe that most of Darwin's population had to be evacuated. There was no food, no power and no drinkable water. People who were able to do so drove south to Adelaide River, Tennant Creek and Katherine. Thousands of others were airlifted in both civilian and military aircraft to cities in the south. After Cyclone Tracy, Darwin was rebuilt, with buildings constructed to withstand cyclones. People returned. Darwin has not experienced a cyclone of Tracy's force since, but weather forecasters say it is not a matter of 'if' but a matter of 'when' it will occur.

Cyclone Larry, 2006

On the morning of 20 March 2006, Cyclone Larry struck the North Queensland coast, near Innisfail. People knew Larry was coming and they were able to prepare and protect themselves. However, they could not protect Queensland's largest crop - bananas. What turned Larry from a cyclone into a natural disaster was the destruction of more than 90 per cent of Australia's banana crop.

Australians eat more than 15 million bananas each week, but for nine months after Cyclone Larry, the supply of bananas crashed. The small number available for sale came from New South Wales, the Northern Territory and Western Australia they became very expensive. Australia does not import bananas because of the threat of disease. People in the industry were laid off work and crop losses were estimated to be $350 million. The total damage bill from Cyclone Larry was $1.5 billion.

NAMING CYCLONES

A Queensland government meteorologist, Clement Wragge, first began naming cyclones in 1887. The practice stopped in 1902 and began again in 1963. Cyclones were given female names until 1975, when male and female names began to be alternated.

CYCLONE YASI, 2011

Early on 3 February 2011 Tropical Cyclone Yasi made landfall in far north Queensland, bringing 285 kilometre per hour winds. Yasi was the costliest cyclone to ever hit Australia, with damage exceeding $3.5 billion.

FLOODS

Floods are an important part of many ecosystems. In Australia, the areas that border the Murray River and the great Macquarie Marshes in New South Wales need to be regularly flooded in order to keep them healthy. Floods become natural disasters when they are so severe that they cause environmental damage, destroy crops and stock, damage buildings, roads and bridges, and take lives.

Different Kinds of Floods

Floods occur in all parts of Australia, from the arid interior to the wet tropics. In northern regions of the country, most floods occur between November and May, as a result of cyclones bringing heavy rain. In southern areas, floods tend to occur more often in winter and spring. However, floods do not follow timetables and may occur at any time due to unusual weather events.

Heavy rainfall can cause creeks and rivers to become swollen with large volumes of water. A flood occurs when this water breaks the banks and spreads out across the land. Floods of this kind can cover large areas and cause crop and livestock losses, as well as damage to bridges, roads and property. Towns built close to rivers can be inundated. Sometimes, these floods can be tracked as rising rivers flow towards towns, and precautions such as building levee banks and sandbagging can be undertaken. A flood may occur many days after heavy rainfall upstream. In the inland of Australia, the irregular flooding of the normally dry Lake Eyre can happen many months after rainfall hundreds of kilometres away send the flood waters on their way.

HIGHEST RAINFALL

The wettest place in Australia is Tully, which is located south of Cairns, in north-eastern Queensland. Tully's annual rainfall is approximately 4,490 millimetres. The nearby town of Babinda recorded higher rainfall than Tully in 2007. The highest recorded rainfall over a 24-hour period was on 3 February 1893, at Crohamhurst in south-east Queensland,when 907 millimetres of rain fell that day.

STORM DAMAGE

Emergency Management Australia, a government body, says that the most damaging natural hazard in Australia, in terms of financial losses, is severe thunderstorms. Most of the damage is caused by hailstones and flash flooding. One hailstorm in Sydney on 14 April 1999 caused more than $ 1.5 billion damage.

LA NIÑA

A pattern known as La Niña Southern Oscillation occurs every three to five years, and has the opposite effect to El Niño Southern Oscillation. La Niña means 'the girl' in Spanish. La Niña brings higher than average rainfall. Floods are more likely to occur during La Niña periods and droughts during El Niño periods.

FLASH FLOOD ALERT!

One of the most destructive kinds of flood is the flash flood. Flash floods happen in local areas and are the result of sudden, very heavy rain, usually associated with thunderstorms. They are especially destructive in cities where drainage systems fail, and streets and houses are threatened with rushing water. The force of this water can be extraordinary. It is not unusual for cars and trucks to be swept away. The Australian Bureau of Meteorology estimates that floods cost the community more than $400 million each year.

AUSTRALIA'S WORST FLOODS

Damaging localised flooding is a regular occurrence in most parts of Australia. Some floods are so devastating that their effects are felt far and wide, and are remembered for many years afterwards.

The Maitland Flood, February 1955

Between 1954 and 1956, Australia's weather was influenced by a La Niña event. There was heavy rainfall over many parts of eastern Australia during this time. On 23 February 1955, the Hunter River in New South Wales was swollen with rainwater and run-off from ground that had been wet for weeks. The river burst its banks and roared into the town of Maitland, in the Hunter Valley.

It was not just Maitland that was affected by this massive flood. The water spread over an area almost twice the size of Tasmania. Photographs and film footage of the devastation in Maitland shocked Australians everywhere. Fourteen people died in Maitland, including five who were electrocuted. Another 11 people died in other flood-affected areas. The damage has been estimated at more than $1.3 billion. The flood of 1955 remains the largest flood to affect the Hunter Valley.

Katherine Floods, January 1998

On 25 January 1998, rain began falling in the area around Katherine in the Northern Territory. The rain was a result of tropical Cyclone Les, which had begun the previous day over the waters of the Gulf of Carpentaria. The rain was heavy, but more importantly it fell continuously for two days. The Katherine, Roper and Daly rivers were swollen with the more than 420 millimetres of rain that had fallen over 48 hours. These rivers were already carrying large volumes of water due to earlier, heavy rainfall. The region's average January rainfall is 236 millimetres. In January 1998, 913 millimetres of rain was recorded. Katherine had begun to flood even before the river rose. Stormwater drains burst and instead of carrying water away, spilled it into the streets. The Katherine and Daly rivers finally broke their banks. More than 1,000 square kilometres of land was flooded. The effect on Katherine was catastrophic. The whole of the central business district was flooded, with water in the main street rising to a depth of two metres. Houses and businesses were devastated, with more than 5,000 people forced to evacuate their premises. An estimated 1,200 homes and 500 businesses were flooded. There were heavy losses in the beef, vegetable and mango industries. Among the expected dangers of disease, food shortages and fast-flowing objects, Katherine's rescuers also had to be wary of snakes and crocodiles. Dangerous snakes were flushed out of their hiding places and swam to dry ground, and crocodiles were washed into Katherine by the floodwaters. Three people died because of the floods, with damage estimated at $70 million.

QUEENSLAND FLOODS, 2010-2011

Beginning in December 2010 and continuing into 2011, a series of floods devastated parts of Queensland. Flooding was so bad that torrents of water flowed into the Lockyer Valley which was described as an inland tsunami.

35 people died and approximately 200,000 people were affected across 90 towns, with 94 suburbs of Brisbane flooded. Three-quarters of Queensland was declared a disaster zone.

EARTHQUAKES

When earthquakes affect built-up areas such as crowded cities, they are among the most devastating natural disasters, with high rates of death and injury.

How do Earthquakes Happen?

The surface of the Earth is made up of large separate plates, called tectonic plates. These are not stable. They shift and move, and when they do, they grind against, or collide with, neighbouring plates. The resulting energy that is released is called seismic energy, which moves in waves from deep in the Earth to the surface. Some seismic waves are so powerful that they cause extensive damage, while others have little effect and go unnoticed.

Seismic activity can occur at any point on the Earth's surface, but there are some regions where earthquakes occur more frequently. These are places where tectonic plates meet. More than 80 per cent of earthquakes occur along a region called the circum-Pacific seismic belt. Countries most affected are New Zealand, Fiji, Papua New Guinea, the Philippines, Japan, the east coast of Russia and the west coasts of Canada, and North and South America. Australia, which is considered to be geologically stable, does not sit on these boundaries, but this does not mean that earthquakes do not happen here. Earthquakes that occur in places that sit in the middle of plates, rather than at the edges, are called 'intra-plate earthquakes'.

MEASURING EARTHQUAKES

Earthquakes are measured using an instrument called a seismograph. The seismograph records vibrations, by measuring the time between different seismic waves, determining the place where the earthquake began, called the 'epicentre'. Earthquakes are measured on the Richter scale, which indicates the magnitude, or size, of the earthquake.

EFFECTS OF EARTHQUAKES

Minor earthquakes cause little or no damage. Earthquakes that take place under the ocean can generate tsunami, which are rapidly moving, giant waves that can cause great destruction to coastal communities.

In towns and cities, earthquakes cause buildings to collapse, and most people die as a result of being crushed, or hit by falling debris. Earthquakes cause landslides under which houses can be buried, and they cause fires that start when gas lines are broken, or when fuels or chemicals are spilled. These fires can burn out of control particularly if the earthquake has disrupted the water supply.

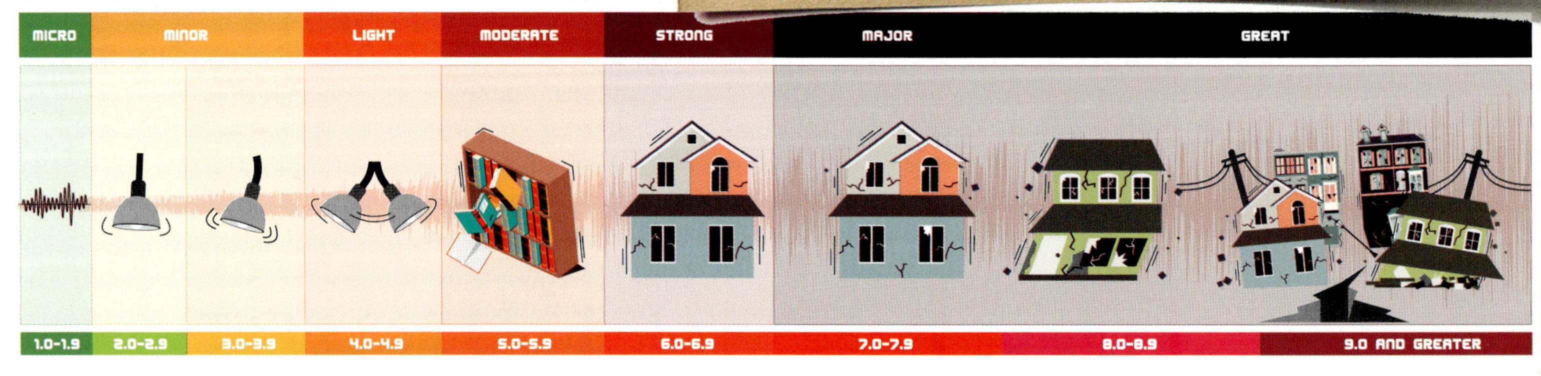

ARE THERE EARTHQUAKES IN AUSTRALIA?

Australia is not known as a continent that suffers large and devastating earthquakes, but like every other place on Earth, earthquakes do occur here, and more regularly than people think. The majority of these earthquakes are tremors that register very low on the Richter scale. Australia has experienced several destructive earthquakes since European settlement.

Newcastle, 28 December 1989

Newcastle is a large city with a population of 144,375 and located to the north of Sydney in New South Wales. At 10.27 am on 28 December 1989, an earthquake struck the city and caused widespread destruction. It also claimed the lives of 13 people. This was the first earthquake recorded in Australia to result in fatalities. The Newcastle earthquake registered 5.6 on the Richter scale — a moderate earthquake. Earthquakes of this size occur regularly in Australia, but they generally occur in areas where the population is small, and where buildings are not densely constructed. The death toll in Newcastle was the result of buildings not being constructed in such a way as to withstand earthquakes. The toll might have been much higher if the earthquake had struck at a different time. School holidays meant that school buildings, many of which were damaged, were empty.

At the Newcastle Workers Club, nine people died when a floor collapsed. A concert was due to be performed at the Club that night and more than 1,000 people were expected. Three people died when the awning of the Kent Hotel in the inner suburb of Hamilton collapsed on them. One other person in Newcastle died as a result of shock. There were fewer people than usual in central Newcastle that day, because a strike by bus drivers meant that public transport was not running at normal capacity. Damage was estimated at more than $4 billion, and 160 people were injured. Three hundred buildings had to be demolished and 50,000 buildings were damaged. The majority being private dwelling homes. The earthquake was felt within an 800-kilometre circle from its epicentre.

AFTERSHOCKS

After a large earthquake, the area in which it occurred settles and continues to shift until it stabilises itself. This results in aftershocks, which are like echoes of the original earthquake. Aftershocks can cause as much damage as, and sometimes more damage than, the actual earthquake. Aftershocks can occur within hours, days, weeks or even months after an earthquake.

AROUND THE WORLD

Globally, there have been countless natural events that have had a devastating impact on the environment and on the people who live there. The myths and tales of ancient civilisations all contain references to devastating geological events. Three of the worst natural disasters are:

1. Central China Floods

The worst natural disaster ever recorded was the 1931 Central China Floods. An estimated 3.7 million people died from drowning, disease and starvation, and a further 50 million people were impacted.

2. Boxing Day Tsunami

On 26 December 2004, the third largest earthquake ever recorded occurred in the Indian Ocean off Sumatra, Indonesia. It unleashed a devastating tsunami that killed 230,000 people across 14 countries and caused untold devastation. Hardest hit was Indonesia where 168,000 people were killed.

3. Haiti Earthquake

In 2010, a catastrophic earthquake hit Haiti, which included weeks of devastating aftershocks. Millions of people were impacted by the quake and death toll estimates ranged from 100,000 to 160,000.

GLOSSARY

arid region - a very dry area

atmosphere - the gases that surround the Earth

civilian - a person who is not a member of the military

climate - the weather conditions in a particular area

climate change - a change in the usual climate patterns

commemorate - to remember

commission - a board of inquiry

debris - rubbish, the result of destruction

drought relief - financial help from the government when a drought is declared

duration - the period of time that something takes

ecosystem - a natural system that supports life within it

electrocute - to kill with an electric shock

El Niño Southern Oscillation - a disruption of the normal ocean currents, air pressure systems and sea surface

eligible - having the right requirements

embers - burning particles

equator - an imaginary line that runs around the Earth and is equally distant from the North and South Poles

evacuate - to leave an area in an emergency

fatalities - deaths

geographical - having to do with a place's location

geologically - having to do with rocks

germinate - to begin to grow

global warming - an increase in the normal annual temperature range of the Earth

greenhouse gases - that cause global warming

species - a class of things with similar characteristics

subtropical - lying outside the tropical zone and between the Tropics of Cancer and Capricorn

suppressant - a substance used to smother or keep down a fire

tectonic plates - slowly moving plates that form the Earth's surface

topsoil - the rich soil in which plants grow

tropics - those areas on or near the Equator

INDEX

FURTHER INFORMATION

Using the Internet

Explore the Internet to find out more about topics discussed in this book. Use a search engine, and type in keywords like 'drought', 'cyclones', 'earthquakes' and the names of the people and events you are interested in.

http://www.bom.gov.au/cyclone/about/intensity.shtml
https://www.ag.gov.au/EmergencyManagement/Pages/default.aspx